IMAGES
of Scotland

NORTH GLASGOW

Mr W.B. Milne poses with his family and staff outside his shop at 329 Springburn Road, between Keppochhill Road and Gourlay Street, on a day of celebration according to the newspaper headlines. Pretoria, the capital city of Transvaal, has surrendered to Lord Roberts' Army on September 1900, but unfortunately the Boer War continued for another two years and the end came under the command of Lord Kitchener. Inside the window is an advert for Crane's Fireworks and at the bottom are a huge selection of briar and clay pipes. Mitchell's Prize Crop cigarettes and the Golden Cut Bar for pipe smokers were locally manufactured, and Stephen Mitchell bequeathed a large sum of money to Glasgow Corporation in 1874 to finance a reference library, now known as the Mitchell, which is the largest municipal owned library in Europe.

IMAGES
of Scotland

NORTH GLASGOW

Andrew Stuart

First published 1998

Reprinted 2001, 2004, 2006, 2008

Tempus Publishing Limited
Cirencester Road, Chalford
Stroud, Gloucestershire GL6 8PE
www.thehistorypress.co.uk

British Library Cataloguing in Publication Data.
A catalogue record for this book is available from the British Library.

ISBN 978 0 7524 1540 6

Typesetting and origination by Tempus Publishing Limited.
Printed and bound in England.

Contents

Acknowledgements

I wish to thank several friends and colleagues who have helped me by lending photographs and postcards from their collections. First of all to Peter Stewart, who photographed Maryhill during 1958 to 1960 and who greatly encouraged me. He also loaned some postcards as did my other colleague, Guthrie Hutton, both of the Strathclyde Postcard Club. My thanks also are given to Willie Gilmartin and his late father for their contributions. I am very grateful to Michelle Rodgers for her photographs. The staff of Springburn Museum have always been very helpful, especially Susan Scott, Designer and Photographer, and the Curator, Dr Gilbert T. Bell, who has granted permission to feature photographs as well as others from the late W. Douglas McMillan's tramcar collection of the fifties. Finally, I thank my son Alan, (and Alan Gallacher), who has assisted me in word processing the text of this book.

Peter Stewart :- Cover Page 29t, 30t, 31, 32b, 33b, 34, 39, 40b, 42b, 43, 44t, 45t, 46b, 54, 56, 59b, 84t, 118.

Guthrie Hutton :- 65b, 66t. Michelle Rodgers :- 27, 68b.

Willie Gilmartin :- 17b, 21t, 26t, 44b, 47t, 48, 49, 59t, 68t, 74t, 76t, 86b, 89, 104, 105t, 110, 112t.

Springburn Museum :- 2 10b, 20t, 91, 92, 99t, 100, 102b, 106b, 108t, 119, 121, 122, 123.

W. Douglas McMillan :- 61, 64b, 76b, 77t, 80, 94, 97, 108b, 112b, 113t.

Introduction

Before the introduction of postal codes, the north of Glasgow was addressed as N1, N2 and NW for Springburn, Possilpark and Maryhill respectively. There was no NE, but the northern part of the vast E3 should have been so designated. There was such a diversity of industry in these working class districts, in fact everything from matchsticks to hundred ton locomotives were manufactured, and quite a few factories had over a thousand employees on their payroll. Workers sought to be near their workplace and stayed within these close knit communities, which endeavoured to have as many amenities around them. Churches, schools, public halls, libraries, wash-houses, cinemas and parks as well as public baths and swimming pools. Most people resided in four-storey sandstone tenements with three or four families living on each landing in one or two apartments and sharing the same WC on the stairway. These circumstances eventually caused overcrowding and insanitary conditions. There was of course, better accommodation available, consisting of two, three or four apartments, all with inside WC, and some even had a bath, but all were at higher rents. All homes were heated by coal-fires and the emission of heavy smoke from countless household chimneys and from those of nearby factories, coupled with a dampish climate, caused these tenements to become blackened with dirt and grime. All of these districts have become smokeless zones and the tenements that are still standing have been stone-cleaned, looking resplendent in the sunshine and not too bad in rain as well. New industries boomed when the Forth and Clyde Canal was opened for traffic in 1790, with much of the northern districts benefiting from the extensive trade in goods shipped from one part of the country to the other. Factories and warehouses were erected on the canal banks. Another industrial use for the canal was in the seasoning of timber logs and sawmills that were situated nearby to take advantage of this. The advent of railways resulted in much the same impact and Springburn in particular was most fortunate in having the workshops and running sheds of two major railway companies, as well as two locomotive builders within their area. Other successful work was in the local iron foundries and a close look at the Edwardian postcards for lamp standards, tramwire support columns, gates, fences, bandstands and fountains show not only their sturdiness but also how decorative they were. Engineering, oils, paints and chemicals were also manufactured and the products were often exported all over the world from Glasgow's docks on the Clyde. Glaswegians were fond of saying that Glasgow made the Clyde, and the Clyde made Glasgow. Working standards, however, in the factories and workplaces, were far from ideal and accidents were frequent as the minimum protection was given to the workforce from machinery, tools and from the handling of hazardous materials. Under various Police and Public

Health Acts, as well as other local and general statutes, the Corporation was the Municipal Authority of the City and owned the utilities of water, gas, electricity, markets, transport and other undertakings. The transport consisted of tramways, subway and bus services around the City. A wave of nostalgia and a tear in the eye comes to older Glaswegians whenever tramcars are mentioned. They were everywhere as can be readily seen in the Edwardian postcards and in the photographs of the late W. Douglas McMillan. Unfortunately in the post-war years, tramcars were mainly responsible for the slow movement of traffic in the mis-named rush hours, and they were all scrapped by September 1962. On a very rainy day on 4 September of that year, quarter of a million people turned out to witness the farewell procession of the tramcars. Thereafter the problem was to be resolved by the building of motorways and access roads to them. Many tenements, old or otherwise, were torn down in the northern districts as a result of building these fast roads. However, as the number of car owners increases, the traffic problems can be chaotic at times, and a ban on private cars into the city centre seems to be inevitable. An ambitious scheme to introduce a light rail system across Glasgow to be partly financed by the Millennium Fund was turned down and so it is back to the drawing board for another try. The heavy industries will never return, and light ones have gone to the overspill towns Glasgow helped to create and is regretting, especially so since the abolition of the Strathclyde Regional Council. Glasgow has always been changing, and whatever the next century may bring the City will always live up to its motto, 'Let Glasgow Flourish'.

One

North Woodside

The area portrayed was triangular in shape with the focal point being St George's Cross northwards to Garscube Road, from there to Queen's Cross and from St George's Cross again and up the former New City Road to Queen's Cross. St George's Cross was a very busy junction with traffic coming from and going to the city centre from the West End, Maryhill, Possilpark and Springburn. All kinds of shops were in abundance here, the most notable being the big store of Wood and Selby, an early aquisition of the House of Fraser. Apart from a few terraced houses off St George's Road, the majority of houses were four-storey tenement blocks, many of which are now demolished in that intensive redevelopment of the late sixties when motorways and access to them were given priority over people. New houses were eventually erected and these are two and three-storey brick-built ones that are attractive enough to be given awards. The industries of the district were food processing, confectionery, foundries, engineering and large warehouses storing spirits and ale. Much of these have been dispersed elsewhere, and only small industrial units and car showrooms are in their stead.

Several types of transport are shown at St George's Cross in 1903, with two open-topped tramcars, a horse and cart going towards Charing Cross, a cyclist on his way out west and a barrow at the kerbside. The columned building in the centre is still standing, but the tenements attached on either side have been demolished.

To the left of the tramcar was the Empress Theatre, which opened in August 1913 and was demolished in 1987. Renamed the Metropole in 1962, the theatre came under the ownership of Jimmy Logan, the celebrated comedian, in 1964. Unfortunately the advent of television and the public's reluctance to venture this far from the city centre caused its closure in 1972.

In May 1958, this tramcar on route 16 has passed St George's Cross and the corner shop drapery of D.M. Hoey, founded in 1898. Their offices were above the shop and had another branch nearby. In the massive upheaval in the late sixties, this family concern transferred its business across the river to Victoria Road, at Crosshill.

The City Bakeries had shops and tearooms scattered about Glasgow. The luxurious ones, like this in St George's Road, also had a restaurant which could be hired out for special receptions. The host would be responsible for the provision of liquor and the entertainment.

The workshops of the bakeries were in the nearby Clarendon Street. In this 1936 photo, ladies are handling mutton pies on to trays which would be van-delivered to their shops. Hot pies, peas, and chips were teatime favourites with many Glasgow families. Famished football fans also devoured them at half-time, washed down with hot Bovril in wintertime and with Irn-Bru in the summer.

Opened in 1897, this was the central premises of the St George Co-operative Society Ltd in their Golden Jubilee year of 1920. This Society was formed on 30 December 1870 by a group of twenty nine men from the Grove Park weaving factory. Their first shop was at 398 St George's Road and eventually there were branches in all the surrounding districts, extending into Anderston, Partick and Whiteinch.

Despite being named after England's patron saint, the educational committee of St George decided that a pipe band should be formed for the society. Here the youthful band poses for a 1920 photograph in the backcourt of the central premises.

In their Golden Jubilee celebrations, the Society held a concert and social evening on 22 December 1920 in the St Andrew's Halls, which was packed to capacity. All their choirs performed including the juvenile and junior ones, who were photographed earlier on the steps at Park Gardens.

At the top of the central premises in Gladstone Street was a sculptured statue of St George slaying a dragon. Before the building was demolished in the late seventies, this was removed and stored for future use, but the date-stone 1897 and the society's name plaque became part of the rubble.

The statue was placed at the re-aligned cross before 1990, the year when Glasgow was the Cultural Capital of Europe. This is floodlit at night and is surrounded by cast-iron railings which were once around the public conveniences at the old cross.

Mr Andrew Carnegie gifted the sum of £100,000 to Glasgow Corporation for the provision of fourteen district libraries in May 1901. Half of these were designed by the same architect, James R. Rhind. They were Woodside, Maryhill, Dennistoun, Bridgeton, Parkhead, Govanhill and Hutchesontown, all built in classical style. Woodside is considered to be the most attractive with fluted Ionic columns, sculptured panels and on top of a dome, statues of a woman and children. The reading rooms were opened on 10 March 1905. Because of cut backs and repairs, Woodside is one of the three libraries which may close in the near future.

St George's in the Fields church, located at 485 St George's Road, was built in 1886 and the architects were Hugh and David Barclay. The sculptured work above the doorway represents Christ dividing the five loaves and ten fishes, and is by Wm. Birnie Rhind. The church was dissolved on 30 June 1980, and this List A building was sold and converted to luxury housing in 1988.

Where St George's Road meets Garscube Road is known as the Round Toll and once was heavily populated as can be seen in this Edwardian postcard. The area was cleared of these tenements and new ones were erected in St George's Road in 1965-6. The rest of the Round Toll was re-aligned for faster traffic and a small industrial estate.

This Edwardian postcard shows a top covered tram followed by a horse and cart going into the continuation of New City Road, which was later designated Maryhill Road. The bank at the corner was taken over by Andrew Massey and Company, one of Glasgow's successful grocery chains in the period between the two world wars.

This Coronation tramcar was on route 18 to Springburn and was passing the bygone Thistle Bar, one of the local pubs where supporters of Partick Thistle Football Club would drown their sorrows more often than to the celebrations of their infrequent victories. The tenements have long since disappeared and are now replaced by new housing.

Two views of Seamore Street at the beginning of this century. The top one was from St George's Cross and on to Maryhill, whilst the bottom went towards the Cross and into the city centre. The tramcars were electrified horse trams with the top deck open to all weathers. All the tenements on the top postcard were knocked down and replaced with brick-built two and three- storey housing. The billboards and shops have also gone and new houses are at present being built there. The tenements in the bottom view have been renovated and stone-cleaned.

Napiershall Street is now a mixture of refurbished sandstone tenements and new brick ones, which replaced those torn down. The vacant school of 1900 is used for business and community purposes and the cast-iron gates, railings and lamp standards have been retained. The spire is that of St Mary's Episcopal Cathedral of 1871-4 in Great Western Road.

This church is located in Raeberry Street and at the corner of Kirkland Street. The Revd D.R. Kilpatrick and 274 members moved from Lyon Street to form a congregation here as North Woodside Free Church in 1875, and their church and halls were ready for worship in 1878. Later they became North Woodside United Free Church and continue as such today.

At the corner of New City Road and Hopehill Road was another popular pub, Ye Olde Tram Car Vaults, which had a model single decker tram as its pub sign. At the other street corner was the Seamore Picture House, (1913-1963), belonging to A.E. Pickard, the millionaire owner of many local cinemas and properties.

The model tramcar went missing sometime after the pub's closure. It was sold for a small sum to an antique dealer who knew of its history. He then handed this over to the People's Palace in Glasgow Green and it went on display there.

The tenement buildings, from North Woodside Road to Napiershall Street, which can be seen behind this tramcar, have survived and have been greatly enhanced by renovation. Taking the place of Ye Olde Tram Car Vaults is a very modern car salesroom which specialises in the sale of Jaguar cars and has their marque enlarged on a pedestal at the entrance.

From the early sixties onwards, gable end murals were very popular in certain districts and this one is on the southern side of the Central Hall built in 1923. This signifies the change from the Methodist Meeting Place to that of a Communal Centre of the seventies for local clubs, craft groups and instruction classes, including one for the tuition of belly dancing.

This design on the other side of the Community Hall was the first 1990 commission for the Cultural Capital programme. It was unveiled by HRH Princess Anne on 4 January 1990. The artist was Daniel Trevor from Clwyd North Wales, with the sponsors being Tay Homes and the Community Central Hall.

Most of the gable end murals have disappeared due to demolition or the modernisation of the tenements. This 1977 one entitled, 'Red, Black and Green, Maryhill Soft Space Shuttle', was at 54 Ancroft Street and the artist was Tim Armstrong. This area was cleared and is now laid out for new houses.

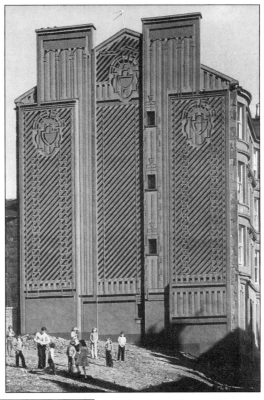

This mural was designed from a drawing by a local schoolgirl and called 'Sunshine and Clouds'. It is now half hidden by new housing in Northpark Street.

This is where Garscube Road met New City Road and became Queen's Cross. The bar at the gushet was the Queen's Cross Vaults, an old fashioned pub used mainly on football match days. It was good for a quick exit, having two doorways in each of the roads.

Partick Thistle FC, founded in 1876, flitted around several grounds in Partick before finally settling outside the district at Firhill. Their successes have been limited. A Scottish Cup win in 1921 against Rangers and the league cup win against Celtic in 1971. This season, 1997/98, was disastrous as they were relegated to Division 2. This superb Ardath cigarette card shows the team in 1936 with the legendary Peter 'Ma Ba' McKennan, 2nd left in the front row.

PARTICK THISTLE F.C.

Above is the perspective drawing of St Matthew's United Free Church at Queen's Cross, submitted by the architect Charles Rennie Mackintosh. This was completed in 1899 at 870 Garscube Road, and described as 'Art Noveau Gothic'. It is now the headquarters of the C.R. Mackintosh Society and is open to visitors by contacting the society for details. Another Mackintosh building that can be seen by appointment is the nearby Ruchill Church Hall.

The trolley bus was introduced to Glasgow in 1949 and lasted for eighteen years, being the briefest spell of public transport in the city, compared with the ninety years of tramcars, a subway system since 1896 and bus services since 1924. Queens Cross was the northern terminal for the 105 route with Clarkston, the southern one. Both were handy for football fans going to Firhill, Hampden and Cathkin.

QUEEN'S CROSS, GLASGOW.

The cross was where New City Road formerly ended, as did Garscube Road to become Gairbraid Street in those Edwardian days. This is now the Maryhill Road of today and those tenements shown are still standing and modernised. However, south of here most houses and industrial units in both these roads are new brick ones, built from 1978 onwards in the redevelopment of the area.

Two

Maryhill

Mary Hill, the owner of the Gairbraid Estate, feued land to the Forth and Clyde Canal Company on condition that her name be given to the town, which she hoped would result from the development of this enterprise. The Canal Company constructed five locks, a drydock and basin and the magnificent four-arched aqueduct over the River Kelvin. A village sprung up near the drydock and the area was first known as The Dock, followed by the Drydock, and then The Kelvin Dock. Early industries were bleaching, calico printing and coal mining. The first two lasted until midway through the nineteenth century, but mining proved to be uneconomical as the pits had to be constantly drained of water. Other industries took over such as boat building, sawmills, foundries, engineering, gasworks, chemical plants and many others. With the building of railway lines to here and beyond, the population upsurged and as a result of lawlessness, the local residents petitioned that Maryhill become a Police Burgh. This was granted in 1856. Twenty years later, Maryhill Barracks were completed for entry and lasted until 1958. The houses for workers were firstly stone cottages and later four-storey tenements were erected. In the thirties and in the post war period, the Corporation of Glasgow built apartment flats and terraced cottages. The biggest change in the area's housing was the building of apartments and high-rise blocks in the Wyndford estate, which was the site of the demolished barracks. The heavy industries have gone and unfortunately Maryhill district is a black spot for high unemployment.

During the Second World War, the railings separating each tenement backcourt were taken away as scrap metal to aid the war effort. They were never replaced, thus making the whole area into one big playground to be enjoyed by children like these wee girls, Irene Dolan, and Lorraine and Michelle Rodgers, snapped in their Maryhill backcourt in 1967.

Two more gable end murals with the cityscape scene off Dalmally Street looking a little drab today and in need of retouching, whilst the geometrical one was covered up by rough casting when this tenement in Maryhill Road was renovated.

The main changes around here since this 1958 photograph was taken are just beyond Dunard Street, at one time the burgh's boundary. The old tenements have been replaced by a modern fire station of 1995, known locally as the 'Mary Hilton'. On the other side, an attractive bridge has been built across the canal into the Student Village in Murano Street.

This model soldier on sentry duty is now on display in the People's Palace. It was formerly placed at the corner of Maryhill Road and Kelvinside Avenue by the owners of the HLI public bar. Behind the bar was a full length mirror with soldiers in various uniforms of that regiment etched upon it.

Emerging from Bilsland Drive on to the main road was the No. 18 tramcar to Burnside, followed into town by the No. 29 to Tollcross. Major road alterations have made this area into a very busy crossroads. The tenements are still standing on this side, but the ones in the other view below have been torn down to make a new entry into Queen Margaret Drive and the West End.

Situated between two tenement blocks in Maryhill Road and round the corner from Bilsland Drive was the oldest cinema in Maryhill, the Star of 1912. Later there were several extensions and after a major refurbishment in 1931, the cinema was renamed the New Star, with seating for 1,800 patrons, an increase of 100%. As the large roof was made up of corrugated steel sheets and not insulated, neighbours and passers-by on the road could hear the soundtrack very clearly. The cinema closed down in 1966 and was replaced by the Milngavie Motors Showroom, which in turn was taken over by new housing of the eighties.

Dr William Mitchell, Vice-Chairman of the Glasgow School Board and a group of zealous ladies and gentlemen set up East Park Home, which was converted from a cottage in 1874, in order to attend to the special needs of infirm children. This became a hospital school for a small number, but increased as the years rolled on and consequently the accommodation was extended. East Park Home is charity funded and maintained by donations and grants.

Until recently, the junior football clubs in the northside competed for the Maryhill Charity Cup with all the proceeds going to the home. In recent times the taxi owners annual outing has taken the children to the Clyde Coast in taxis garlanded in ribbons and balloons with the drivers in fancy dress.

Garrioch Public School was typical of those erected in the last decade of the nineteenth century, a three-storey sandstone building with separate entrances and playgrounds for boys and girls. Discipline was often upheld by the threat of punishment. This would be so many strokes on the palms by a leather tawse, administered by the teacher. In Glasgow parlance, this was 'getting the belt'. The school is now closed and boarded up against vandalism.

This station was used mainly by passengers on the suburban services. These went underground into Glasgow Central low-level station, and were dirty, smoky, and soot encrusted with little ventilation, so a hop on a tramcar was the preferred choice for the traveller. However, the station was convenient for soldiers going on leave, laden with their kitbag and greatcoat, as it was next to the barracks.

This station had several names. Firstly it was Maryhill Barracks, then Caledonian Maryhill and finally after the nationalisation to British Railways, it became Maryhill Central. The station was built in 1896 for the Lanarkshire and Dumbartonshire Railways and had two island platforms connected by a footbridge.

The line closed on 5 December 1964 and amongst the objectors to the closure was the Glasgow Corporation. When the Maryhill Co-op Shopping Centre and car park were constructed in 1980, provision was made underneath for re-opening of the line should this ever be required in the future. McDonalds, Mecca Bingo and small industrial units across the main road have taken the place of the tenement blocks.

In this scene, which is now Maryhill Road, everything on the right has gone and has been replaced by a new police station, a health centre and job centre offices. On the other side, the walls of the barracks are still standing, and inside of the entrance are three solid pillars, grouted into the ground, that were once part of the gates, with the date of 1875 and VR embossed on them.

Maryhill Barracks was built in 1869-76 to replace the old Infantry ones of 1795 in the Gallowgate. The government bought 30 acres of the Garrioch Estate from James Davidson of Ruchill and a further 27 acres before the completion. The Barracks were demolished in 1961 and became the Wyndford Housing Estate, planned and managed by the Scottish Special Housing Association.

The first troops to occupy the barracks were a detachment from the 6th Dragoons, who arrived on 29 April 1877, the '0' Battery of 2nd Brigade, Royal Artillery on 25 October 1877 and the 79th Highlanders on 15 March 1878. This regiment later became the Queen's Own Cameron Highlanders, who left in June the next year for Gibralter.

The Barracks, Maryhill.

The Argyll and Sutherland Highlanders, formerly the 91st Argyllshire and 93rd Sutherland Highlanders, were on guard duty when this photograph was taken. Their first tour of duty here was in 1882 and they were stationed for almost two years before leaving for Portsmouth on 18 July 1884. The guardroom has been retained and is in use as the estate office.

The Highland Light Infantry, (HLI), was raised in 1777 and they are shown here in their uniforms of 1900. The regiment moved to Maryhill Barracks from Hamilton on 16 March 1921. They later became the City of Glasgow's Regiment. The last HLI soldiers to be trained here, left on the 26 September 1958. On 21 January 1959, the HLI amalgamated with the Royal Scots Fusiliers to become the Royal Highland Fusiliers.

The letters GSH, carved above the doorway, signified that this was the Glasgow Soldiers Home, a place of comfort and relaxation for off duty soldiers escaping from the rigours of the barracks. The Home later became the licensed Northern Club of the Glasgow Trades Council and is at present the Frampton Entertainment Centre.

The Roxy, Maryhill's biggest and best cinema, opened *c.* 1930 on the site of a former one, the Maryhill Picture House, which lasted from 1914 to 1929. James Graham was the Roxy's owner and he had other cinemas in Springburn, Possilpark, Townhead and Partick. In the days of cine-variety shows, this was excellent for performers who found favour with the owner and audiences. The cinema continued until 1962, and when the area was redeveloped, there were new shops, DHSS offices and a pub once called the Elephant and Bugle, the emblems on the HLI cap badge. The pub's name was shortened to the Bugle and has a replica of that instrument underneath its name, with the lounge bar called the Tuskers.

Maryhill Burgh Halls, designed by the architect Duncan McNaughtan, was opened on 26 April 1878 with a banquet in the afternoon and a ball in the evening. The Burgh was independent of Glasgow until 1892. Wyndford Street was the continuation of Gairbraid Street, both of which have become the Maryhill Road of today.

There were twenty stained glass panels in the halls, depicting the trades and industries of the region. As these have great social history significance, they were purchased by the Museums and Art Galleries for the People's Palace collection. The halls have been under used since the sixties and entry into Gairbraid Avenue has been sealed off to traffic.

Free Library, Maryhill   RELIABLE SERIES.

This pre-1914 postcard is titled Free Library, Maryhill. This is the smallest of the seven libraries designed by architect James R. Rhind for Glasgow Corporation and financed by Andrew Carnegie's generous grant. Like Woodside there is a sculptured panel above the doorway and statues of a woman reading to two children on the roof of the library, which was opened on 4 September 1905.

The same locality some forty five years later, but without the cast iron fountain and lamp standard which have disappeared. About to step on the zebra crossing are two ladies pushing a zinc bath on a set of pram wheels. Most old folk know that this was the conveyance for taking the washing to and from the public wash house, known in Glasgow as the 'Steamie', which was behind the Burgh Halls.

The Maryhill Football Club of 1896. They were founded in 1884 and are the oldest junior club in the northside of Glasgow. They were the Central League Champions of 1996/97 and they have won the Scottish Cup in 1900 and 1940. Lochburn Park, their home ground, is the most modern in the league, thanks to the generosity of a local businessman, Freddie Duda. Their most famous professionals were David Meiklejohn of Rangers, and Danny McGrain and Tommy Burns of Celtic, who were capped for Scotland fifteen, sixty two and eight times, respectively.

The ex-Liverpool 'Green Goddess' tramcar heads on towards Gairbraid Avenue and passes two-storey houses, now demolished, with steps outside the closemouth, a most unusual feature for houses in Glasgow. On the edge of the pavement, someone has chalked, 'Vote Labour' which was countermanded at that time by the Tory slogan, 'You've never had it so good'.

Robert Whitworth was the engineer in charge of building the canal at Maryhill and the aqueduct through the main road was rebuilt in 1881 to replace a smaller one which became inadequate for the traffic of that time. Unfortunately, during the rush to and from workplaces, today's traffic can clog up here and this may be the reason for those faster alternative roads that have caused so much upheaval. As for pedestrians, the footpaths through the aqueduct are always dampish.

Access to these tenements are in Sandbank Street, formerly Church Street. The nearest block to the church has been demolished but the remainder has been stone-cleaned and modernised. The billboards have been dismantled and a clearer view of Maryhill High church can be seen. The church was built in 1846 and designed by the architect Charles Wilson, (1810-1863).

The Kelvin Dock or Drydock in 1949, where, since 1789, small ships were built and repaired, such as lighters, scows and puffers, those little steam coasters immortalised in the stories of *Para Handy* by Neil Munro. The basin is between locks 22 and 23 of the Maryhill locks, which are five in number.

The Dock Basin some ten years on and the later efforts by the Forth and Clyde Canal Society have fairly tidied up this area. With a huge grant from the Millennium Fund, the canal is to be re-opened and it is the society's aim to make this navigable from Grangemouth to Bowling for leisure, pleasure and perhaps once more for commerce.

Surprisingly, the only item in this Edwardian postcard that is standing today is the Kelvin Dock pub at the corner. All the buildings have been demolished, including the fine looking one on the left. The reason for this devastation was to build another fast road to the western part of Glasgow.

Main Street, like the ones of Gairbraid and Wyndford and part of New City Road, is now known as Maryhill Road. This part of the district from the aqueduct to the horse tram terminus in Duart Street was once the original village. The tramcar already displays Mount Florida on its destination board but has still to reach the Maryhill terminal.

A few years before gambling was legalised, small betting shops such as this one sprung up everywhere. They would be occasionally raided by the police who would lift a few punters, book them at the nearest station and thereafter release them. Their fines would be paid by the bookmaker who also gave thirty shillings to each punter (who was usually an old age pensioner) for the inconvenience caused to them.

Another place of worship in Sandbank Street, formerly Church Street, is St George's Episcopal church, built in 1892 by a local architect, Alexander Petrie. Many of the windows have stained glass panels, including one of Boer War Memorial, of 1901, and three placed there in 1947-50, designed by Margaret Chilton and Marjorie Kemp.

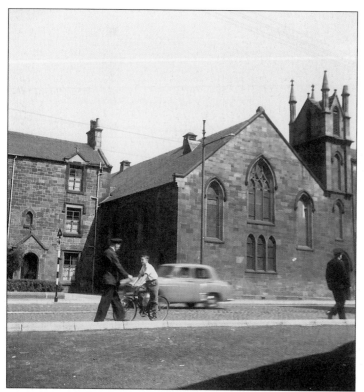

The first chapel of the Immaculate Conception of the Blessed Virgin Mary was erected in 1851 and was adjoined by the Presbytery and halls in Maryhill Road between Duncruin and Kilmun Streets. On the night of an air raid on 14 March 1941, a landmine was dropped on Kilmun Street and killed 107 people. The blast badly damaged the chapel and it wasn't until 1957 that the parishioners were able to worship in a newly built one further out in Maryhill Road.

Main Street was still the shopping centre for locals in this 1958 scene. Galbraith's and the Co-op were for groceries, cakes and scones. Bread could be bought from the home bakeries, fish from the fishmonger and meat from the butcher. Birrell's at the edge on the left was one of the City's main confectioners. Two supermarkets take care of today's customers.

This was Maryhill's tram depot in 1958 which in four years time would be converted into a garage for eighty buses. Tram services once using the depot were No.11 to Battlefield, No.13 to Clarkston, No.23 to Ballieston, No.40 to Ibrox and the last service was No.29 to Tollcross which ended on 22 November 1961. New houses have been built on the garage site.

The main changes between this 1920 postcard and today are on the right. The four-storey tenements in red sandstone have been renovated and the smaller buildings have been knocked down. The solid cast iron lamp standards have also gone. The corner shop sells auto spares and another is a bookie's and sandwiched between them is a newsagent.

Maryhill Hibs were formed in 1924 and they won the Scottish Cup in 1928 by beating Burnbank Athletic, 6 goals to 2. Riley, their inside forward, scored directly from a corner kick. In the thirties they were renamed Maryhill Harp and played at Kelvindale Park in Kilmun Street. In 1955 they transferred two, seventeen year old players to Celtic, Bertie Auld and Dunky McKay, who gained three and fourteen Scottish International caps respectively. The 'Harp' became defunct in 1966 after their ground was taken over for new housing.

50

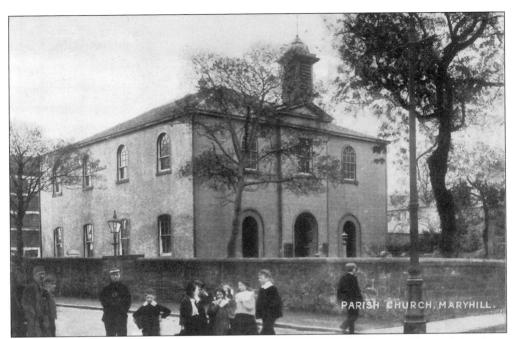

PARISH CHURCH, MARYHILL.

Miss Lilias Graham of Garbraid gifted the grounds wherein Maryhill Parish church of 1825 was erected. The church, which became Maryhill Old, ceased as a place of worship in 1981 and is now in a derelict condition. In the church graveyard there are memorials to local worthies, farmers and merchants. In front of the doorway is a cast iron column which was inscribed to George Miller, a nineteen year old worker who was mortally stabbed by a strike breaker on 24 February 1834 during a calico printing trade dispute.

By an act of Parliament in 1869, the Corporation of Glasgow acquired two local gas companies and was given powers to supply gas to the city and neighbouring surrounds. New works could also be constructed. One of these was Dawsholm, Maryhill, which was erected in 1871 and modified several times as the installations needed renewal and enlargement. The design and erection were to the plans and supervision of the Corporation's Gas Engineer, William Foulis, (1838-1903). Chemical works were built alongside to deal with residual products, which when processed were sold to manufacturers. The gasworks ceased production on 31 March 1964 and the site is now being used for other industries.

Dawsholm works had eleven industrial locomotives, all of which were 0-4-0 saddle tank engines and ran on 4'-8 ½ " gauge rails. They were mostly manufactured by the local locomotive companies such as Dubs, Neilson and Andrew Barclay. Four of them were scrapped whilst the works were still producing and the rest dispersed to other gasworks after the closure. Inside the gasworks and running on a 2ft gauge rail were a number of small locomotives for use in the retort ovens and all of these were scrapped.

Bringing in coal and taking away empty wagons was done by the railway company's goods locomotives. They uncoupled their wagonloads in at the sidings, from which the works saddle tanks would shunt them around as required. This area was excellent for trainspotting and photography if permission was given to do it .

Maryhill Railway Station opened in 1858 for the Glasgow, Dumbarton and Helensburgh railway line to convey passengers and goods between these towns and other stations on the line from Glasgow. It was renamed Maryhill Park when the railways were nationalised in January 1948 and was closed in October 1961. A few years ago, the station was modernised and has re-opened since December 1993 for a commuter, half hourly service between Maryhill and Queen Street Station in Glasgow, stopping at Summerston, Lambhill, Possilpark/Parkhouse and Ashfield.

The industrial school at Maryhill was a residential home for wayward girls and conditions were strict and austere. The annual cost for each inmate in 1890 was £18 8s 10¾d, and there was an average of 225 on the roll. On 1 April 1926, the Glasgow Juvenile Delinquency Board was taken over by the Education Authority and thereafter the school was known as an 'Approved' one. Girls on completion of their stay were occasionally persuaded to take up service in Canada. The building has long since gone.

BAILLIE CLELLAND'S HOUSE, MARYHILL.

This house was called Bonville, built in 1810, and the first owner was Andrew Walker, the proprietor of a local colliery, Sandyflat. Baillie Charles Clelland was the last owner and he lived here all his life. He became a Glasgow Town Councillor when the Burgh of Maryhill was annexed in 1891. Later still he became a Baillie and was the first elected Chairman of the Education Authority. He was also given a knighthood and died in 1941. The house was knocked down in 1948.

The new chapel of the Immaculate Conception was built on the site of Bonville House in 1955-56 and designed by the architect, Thomas S. Cordiner, who was responsible for many chapels built in the post war years. This one was very striking with a huge painting of the Virgin Mary above the doorway and a steep sloping roof structured on concrete 'A' frames. Unfortunately, these were unsound and consequently the building was demolished and replaced by a modest conventional chapel by 1990.

Garscube Estate belonged to the Campbells of Succoth since 1687 and Garscube House was built in 1827 for Sir Archibald Islay Campbell of that ilk. The House and part of the estate were acquired by Glasgow University for their Veterinary Science Department and halls of residence for lecturers and students, but due to dry rot the house was demolished in 1954.

Glasgow Corporation obtained 72 acres of the Garscube Estate in 1921 to be laid out as Dawsholm Park. Football pitches, a pitch and putt course and a children's playground are within the grounds. Most of this park has been left in its natural state and birds and squirrels abound amidst the forest of trees which are mainly of oak and beech.

In his report for 'Municipal Glasgow 1914', James Whitton, Superintendant of Parks, describes Maryhill Park as a small one of 5½ acres which was acquired in 1892. He noted that it served as a quiet retreat for old and young, was of great benefit to the district and much appreciated.

Maryhill Park

The 1974 official handbook of Parks Department describes Maryhill Park as 23 acres and acquired in 1922. A 1921 map shows that the extra ground was the Acre Plantation. The Acre was the name given to the elegant red sandstone villa, built around 1880, for the sole occupancy of the builder, John Watt. He was a partner in the building contractors, Watt and Wilson of Glasgow.

An excellent view near the Maryhill boundary of a No. 29 Corporation tramcar which started its early days in Liverpool and nicknamed there 'Green Godesses'. Glasgow purchased forty six of these between 1953 and 1956, and they were employed on certain routes, 15 and 29, being too long for clearance in some Glasgow streets. However they lasted until withdrawal in 1960, just before the end of the tramcar era in 1962.

As tramcars shoogled their way out of Maryhill and on to Milngavie, a point of interest for travellers was the weather vane mounted on top of a greenhouse in the allotments beside the park. This had the silhouettes of a black cat ready to pounce upon a mouse.

Maryhill Harriers, founded in 1888, is one of the few remaining clubs in the Glasgow region. Here in 1938 John Emmet Farrell was the winner of the National Cross-Country Championship and is carried shoulder high by his winning team colleagues of Maryhill. Sports meetings were once great summer attractions sponsored by Rangers FC and the Glasgow Police, with the biggest cheer going to Dunky Wright, Maryhill Harriers, as he finished the marathon.

The Co-operative Women's Guild had popular meeting nights where craftwork, home baking and talks would be on the programme. Always on show would be the branch's banner, bought and commissioned by their members. Maryhill's banner has a dark blue cloth background with painted details in celebration of their Golden Jubilee.

Three

Lambhill

Lambhill was a small village outwith the boundaries of Glasgow until 1926 when it became part of the big city. Most of the men worked in the nearby coalmines, quarries and foundries and lived in small stone cottages. A pit disaster occurred on 3 August 1913, and twenty two men lost their lives. Fourteen of them were from Lambhill and eleven were members of St Agnes' chapel. They are buried in St Kentigern cemetery, where there is a memorial to the victims. Within the vicinity of the village and across the canal bridge are three cemeteries. Lambhill with a gateway by the architect James Sellars who is buried there, St Kentigern where there are fine memorials to Italian families who came to Glasgow, and the Western Necropolis which is next to Glasgow Crematorium. Lambhill House was built in 1788 by William Graham and his descendants lived there until the early part of this century when the Glasgow Corporation took possession. In 1947 Scottish Special Housing laid out the Cadder Scheme on the lands of Lambhill House. The tenement houses in the village built before 1900 were torn down and replaced by modern flats but the Corporation houses of the thirties and the tenement, known as Mallon's Corner still stand. The wastelands on the eastern side of the district were drained in the early sixties and an industrial estate was formed with the biggest factory being that of the City Bakeries, who moved from Woodside to here around 1970. However, the industries introduced on the new estate have hardly compensated for those of the past that have vanished.

Lambhill didn't have electric tramcars until midway through the first decade of this century. The terminus was at the foot of the village in Drummond Street, now Strachur Street. The first service was route 4b to Linthouse and the last was route 31 to Merrylee on 5 December 1959.

This view of Lambhill is obscured by trees which are now gone and on the knowe itself are tenements built in the late fifties. The old block on the right has been demolished and the rooftop is that of St Agnes' chapel. Between these two was Lambhill's first school of 1884, which is now Balmore Nursery.

Lambhill village at the turn of this century shows the bakery's van-man delivering a breadboard of unwrapped loaves. Cyclists could have stopped at the Rest or continue pedalling on to Possil Loch, (a bird sanctuary), Lambhill and St Kentigern cemeteries or further out to the village of Balmore.

Revd Father James Cameron, who was later appointed Canon, was the Parish Priest of Maryhill for fifty five years and was the founder of St Agnes' parish in Lambhill. This began as a mission and in 1880 St Agnes' school was erected, which was used as a chapel on Sundays. The school was later in use for teaching children with special needs and was renamed St Joan of Arc. It is now the Balmore Nursery. St Agnes' chapel was built in 1894 and the first resident priest was Revd Father Houlihan. The chapel was designed by Pugin and the stonework was hewn from the Locharbrigg quarries in Dumfriesshire.

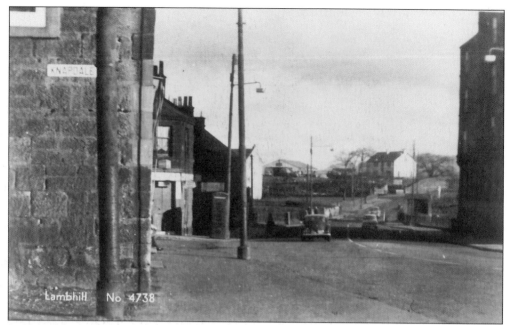

In Knapdale Street, which was formerly Crawford Street, is the Lambhill Mission Hall, which was built in 1907 and is still thriving. Their first mission was on the north side of the canal in the old stables, now used as a car repair workshop. The tramcars have gone in this 1968 image now much changed by the demolition of old buildings for new houses and a new St Joan of Arc school on the right.

This was Crawford Street around 1910 and the cottages were the Cambus Villa, used by Revd Father Houlihan as his presbytery before the building of one within the grounds of St Agnes'. The others were Cambus Cottage and Possil Cottage, occupied by the miners who worked in the local coalfields.

Strachur Street, once called Drummond Street, was not only the tram terminus, but also an oasis on hot summer days because of Acci De Marco's ice cream parlour at the corner. At the other end of the street was the entrance to Lambhill Ironworks, which later became Lambhill Engineering, unfortunately now defunct.

All that remains from this 1910 postcard view is the two-storey block in the middle of the picture. This is now the Handy Stores and Lambhill Post Office. Many old timers will remember when this was Mrs Hannah's sweetie shop. On the right hand side there is now a bookmaker's shop and a lounge bar called, The Inn. After crossing the bridge, a turn into the left leads to the Scottish Special Housing Association scheme called Cadder.

The wooden bridge at the bottom of Lambhill Village was often a meeting place for locals. Any activity on the canal brought great interest, whether this was a cargo barge pulled by a horse on the towpath or one of the passenger steamers on a pleasure trip. The larger building on the left was the horse stables and is now a listed building. The bridge was replaced by a road bridge in 1934 built by Sir William Arrol and Sons Ltd, Bridgeton.

Until the outbreak of the Second World War in 1939, little pleasure steamers plied daily from Port Dundas to Craigmarloch, a few miles beyond Kirkintilloch. One of the most popular was the SS *May Queen*, built in 1903 by P. McGregor and Son of Kirkintilloch. This little vessel carried 231 passengers and was often chartered for works outings and by other organisations. The SS *May Queen* was sold in 1918 to Palmer's Shipbuilding Company, Hebburn-on-Tyne.

Four

Ruchill

The country estates, which are now part of the City of Glasgow, were in the hands of Glasgow merchants. Ruchill was no exception and the owner James Davidson, sold the lands to the Corporation of Glasgow in 1892. Part of this became Ruchill Park and the remainder allotted to the building of a Hospital for Infectious Diseases. This opened on 13 June 1900 and the Ruchill Steam Laundry and Disinfectant Station, adjacent to the hospital, was built at the same time. Industries were at the other end of the district and next to the canal. These were Sandeman's Oil Works of 1880 and Alexander Ferguson's Paint Works of 1874, whose address was once Ruchill Wharf, Forth and Clyde Canal. Still going strong since 1876 is George MacLellan's Rubber Works, whose adverts once declared that they manufactured almost anything in rubber except babies dummy teats. There was also Ruchill Sawmills, which was partly taken over by Bryant and May, (1918 to 1981), who produced the renowned matches, Swan Vestas and Scottish Bluebell. Situated nearby were tenements for the workers and these have been renovated and refurbished. The rest of the district's housing was built by the Corporation in the thirties and much of these have been torn down and replaced by new housing built by various housing associations set up at the beginning of this decade.

This panoramic view shows Ruchill Fever Hospital at the top left and at the right hand side were the chimneys of industrial firms at Firhill. It can be readily seen how steep the grounds of the park from the Firhill entrance were, and they sloped down again to the Bilsland Drive gates.

The Coronation tramcar has passed under the Forth and Clyde Canal aqueduct of 1879 and entered into Bilsland Drive, the main road through Ruchill and on to Possilpark. At the bend where the taxi has passed are steps from Murano Street, and posing on them in 1964 are Mrs Margaret Rodgers with her daughter and grand daughter, Annie and Helen Alexander, and her daughter in law, Kathleen Rodgers.

RUCHILL PARK, GLASGOW.

The Corporation of Glasgow purchased 91 acres of the estate of Ruchill, (a corruption of Roughill) in 1891. A public park of 53 acres was to be laid out by the Superintendent of Parks, James Whitton. An artificial mound with a flagpole on top was made from 24,000 cart loads of earth and nicknamed 'Ben Whitton' by the locals. Excellent views of Glasgow, the Campsies and Ben Lomond can be seen from the mound top on a clear day.

Both these views were at the Firhill entrance to the park and led into well tended gardens and shrubberies. The park is very hilly but this is compensated by the scenic opportunities offered of the surrounding areas. Spion Kop was another name for that artificial mound and was adapted from a Boer War engagement.

This was a most unusual design for a bandstand of 1900 as the majority of them would have been cast iron circular ones from local foundries, especially from the Saracen workshops which were about a mile away. Concert parties and band performances were once great attractions but since the end of World War Two, their popularity had faded. On the day of performance, a flag flew from the flagpole for all to see.

Bowling Greens, Ruchill Park, Glasgow.

Ruchill Park has two bowling greens which are well used in the season and two football pitches, once used by Partick Thistle FC for training purposes. Another of the park's sports amenities was the nearby nine-hole golf course.

At the Bilsland Drive entrance was the children's playground with the usual sturdy equipment. In those bygone days, any misbehaviour by youngsters was held in check by the sharp piercing whistle of the park attendant, or 'parkie' as he was called by them. To have the same effect nowadays would require the services of an SAS regiment!

A Fever Hospital was built on 36¼ acres of the Ruchill estate purchase were for and 1¼ acres used for a washing and disinfecting laundry, both of which were to be built to the plans of the City Engineer, A.B. McDonald. The walls around the hospital were later screened by trees.

This is the only entrance into Ruchill Hospital, on Bilsland Drive. On the wall near to the gatehouse is an ornate bronze plaque commemorating the laying of the foundation stone laid on 29 August 1895 by Lady Bell, the wife of Sir James Bell, Lord Provost of Glasgow. The Hospital for Infectious Diseases was formally opened by Princess Christian on 13 June 1900.

Because of the high ground on which the hospital is situated, it was necessary to erect a water tower which is the hospital's most prominent landmark. It is 165 feet in height, looks like a church bell tower but has no clock faces, unlike several other Glasgow hospitals.

Ruchill's administrative block was a red sandstone one, three-storeys high and provided accommodation for the administration staff and quarters for 200 nurses. The cost of the hospital was £330,000, but this was increased by a further 10% for new phthsis wards. The treatment for all infectious diseases was provided for and a washing and disinfecting station was built within the grounds with a separate gateway in Bilsland Drive. The hospital is now closed and the grounds are on the selling market. The infectious diseases of the last century and the beginning of this one have been almost eradicated by the new treatments and the care of dedicated medical staff. Long may this continue.

The Red Hackle bridge carried the redundant Caledonian Railway's Hamiltonhill Branch Line, whose tracks have been long since uplifted. This bridge, and the close by one in Balmore Road, were demolished in the early seventies. At the other end in Stobhill Road, Springburn, the embankment has been filled in and sited on this is now a supermarket and a car sales complex.

This mural was the only one in Ruchill and the building was knocked down in 1997 in order that a proposed road bypass could be routed from Bilsland Drive to Balmore Road. The mural was in red, black and white and unfortunately an easy target for graffiti.

Five

Possilpark

A couple of miles from the city centre was Possil House, a large mansion within the Possil Estate, and scattered around this were small farms and a few rows of workers cottages. All this was changed from 1869 onwards when Walter MacFarlane, the proprietor of the Saracen Foundry in Anderston, (which had transferred there from the original Saracen Foundry in the Gallowgate), acquired the estate. The mansion was demolished and a new larger Saracen Foundry was laid out. The remainder of the estate was leased for other industries and for building homes for workers. These industries were diverse, structural work for warehouses and tea plantation buildings by A. & J.Main and Brownlie & Murray, machinery for shipyards by Hugh Smith, high tensile bolts and nuts by A.P.Newall, glassmaking by the City Glass Company, fine china and earthenware by the Saracen and Possil Potteries and cardboard box manufacturing by Brownlee and others. Regrettably, all these were closed by the mid-eighties. Tenement blocks were built on both sides of Saracen Street, the main thoroughfare, and in the thirties the Corporation built many houses for the Possil, Keppoch and Hamiltonhill schemes, much of which has been renovated although huge chunks have also been demolished. It is hoped that the regeneration of the district will in time be accomplished.

William McNeil was listed in the post office directories from mid 1920s to late 1930s as a farmer and cartage contractor at the Possil Mains Farm, Ashfield Street. This was situated before the railway line and behind the factory of A. & J. Main. This is now occupied by the British Telecommunications' offices and garage.

This Coronation Mark 11 tramcar has swung from St George's Road into Possil Road and is about to pass the pawnbroker and the High Walk Shoe Company. They sold cheap footwear and had nothing to do with those fashionable platform shoes! When the junction became busier after the demise of the tramcar, the duty policeman was perched high on a wooden platform to direct the flow of traffic.

On 20 October 1956, tramcar No. 174 was approaching the Possil aqueduct of the Forth and Clyde Canal which extended into Port Dundas and joined up with the Monkland Canal. Of particular interest is the billboard for VP wine, translated by some as Vintage Port and by others as Very Potent.

Not only have the tramcars and their cobbled tracks now gone since this 1956 view but so have the tenements on the right. The four-storey ones were built just before the twentieth century and the other was a Glasgow Corporation block of council houses of 1930. The area is now partly landscaped and blighted by large billboards.

The Estate and Craigbank House, (partly seen on the right), were purchased in 1926 by Revd Father McMenemy of St Agnes,' Lambhill. This little chapel of St Teresa was built within these grounds in 1932 and later became the parish halls when the new magnificent St Teresa was dedicated for worship on 8 December 1960, by The Most Revd Donald A. Campbell DD, Archbishop of Glasgow.

The single-storey building on the left was that of Askit Ltd, the manufacturers of well known headache powders. This 1933 building is now the colour printing works of Gavin Watson, Ltd. The other large one was once Greenlees and Son, footwear manufacturers and was the largest reinforced concrete factory in Glasgow at the time of building in 1911. This later became Blindcraft and was demolished in the mid-eighties.

Possilpark School was built in 1890 and lasted until 1966 when a new comprehensive one was erected to accommodate the pupils and also those of Possil High, whose premises were converted into pensioners' flats. Possilpark School is now closed with only the main building remaining. This is called Ardoch House and is used for business and communal purposes.

This corner building was named Tigh Ruadh, (Gaelic for reddish-brown house), and was the residence and surgery of Dr J.S. Muir. The other occupant in Saracen Street was David King, proprietor of Keppoch Iron Works in Ashfield Street. The clergy of St Teresa were the last ones to reside here before the Cowlairs Co-op Society bought it in 1935. There was a lengthy court case before they were allowed to demolish and rebuild on this site.

Cowlairs Co-op Society opened their new emporium here in April 1939. Both sides of Saracen Street had many shops and more than a few belonged to Cowlairs Co-op, which at one time disputed with St George Co-op for the territorial rights to trade in Possilpark. The emporium, by the way, is now a private snooker club.

The last day of route No. 27, Springburn to Renfrew Cross or Shieldhall, was on 15 March 1958. These trams have arrived at Saracen Cross and will continue to the top of the street, turn right into Hawthorn Street and go to straight on to Springburn terminus. The shop on the left is Smith's, a fruiterer, who has been trading here for most of this century.

Saracen Cross was always a busy crossroads and still is despite northern Saracen Street and eastern Bardowie Street being sealed off for through traffic. Of particular interest on the extreme right is the entrance to the local picture house, fondly remembered as the wee Possil and latterly as the Avon. A public house and a large lounge bar now occupy the same site.

This reproduction of a fountain canopy was placed in Bardowie Street in 1987 and could be regarded as a poor substitute for those manufactured at the local Saracen Foundry. In the mid-sixties the Glasgow Corporation City Council decided that all cast-iron bandstands and fountains were too costly to maintain and scrapped all but a few of them.

In the fifties the shops competing for trade against the Co-op were the grocers, Galbraith, Massey and Templeton, all of which became the Allied Grocers Ltd and were taken over by a national supermarket chain. Shoe shops were Easiephit, Greenlees and Tyler, whilst the fishmonger was Agnew, Mc Manus was the draper and Forrester's Stores sold hardware and bric-a-brac. Italians ran the ice cream parlours and fish 'n' chip shops. No curry or kebab carry-outs were to be seen.

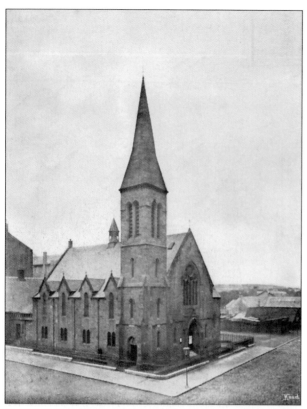

A mission at the top of Saracen Street was the start for Possilpark church in 1877. Ground was acquired in Bardowie Street at Ardoch Street and the church hall was ready in 1879, whilst the church was completed for worship in 1886. By 1892 this was known as Possilpark Parish and had a congregation roll of 450 which increased to 1,000 in the thirties. In April 1975 Possilpark united with Rockvilla and worshipped in the latter which was demolished in 1986. This was rebuilt as Possilpark on the same site in 1988.

At the corners of Allander and Barloch Streets stood the Possilpark Free Church since 1881. This was later renamed the Henry Drummond Memorial after the Glasgow University Professor who conducted regular service therein. He lived nearby in Craigbank House and Estate. The congregation united with Trinity Possil in Broadholm Street on 8 June 1967 and thereafter the old church was torn down and replaced with new housing.

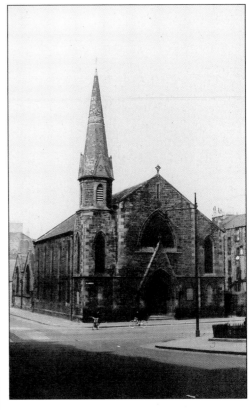

The Saint Matthew Episcopal church building at Balmore Road was completed in 1937, but the ministry has been in Possilpark since 1895. The manse was gifted by the minister some years ago as a centre to assist the rehabilitation of drug addicts and their families and is called 'The Place'.

Possil House

Sir Archibald Alison, Sheriff of Glasgow, rented Possil House from 1835 to 1867, and amongst his famous visitors were Charles Dickens, Sir Colin Campbell, (Lord Clyde), and the Crown Prince of Denmark. Possil House and the estate were bought by Walter MacFarlane in 1869 and he built his third Saracen Foundry there, set up the district of Possilpark and leased the remaining acreage to other industrialists.

Saracen Foundry was world famous for architectural cast-iron work and while much of their exported work has survived, the only remaining examples in Glasgow are the Fountain in Alexandra Park, another in Glasgow Green and decorative lamp standards outside the People's Palace.

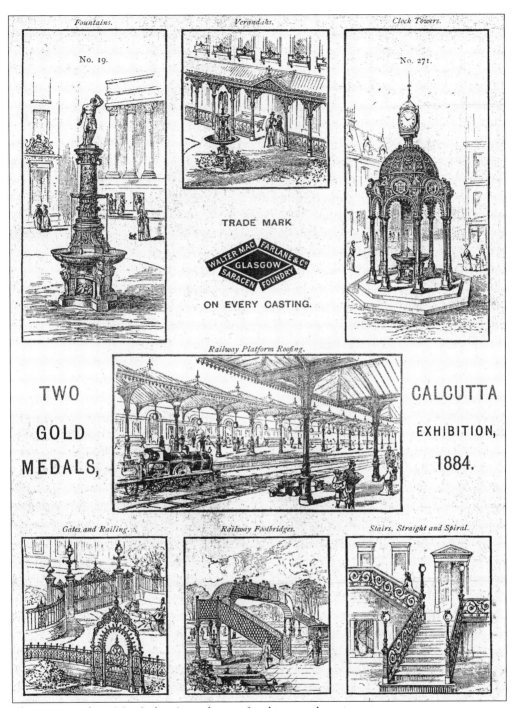

Fountains.

No. 19.

Verandahs.

Clock Towers.

No. 271.

TRADE MARK

WALTER MAC FARLANE & C°
GLASGOW
SARACEN FOUNDRY

ON EVERY CASTING.

Railway Platform Roofing.

TWO
GOLD
MEDALS,

CALCUTTA
EXHIBITION,
1884.

Gates and Railing.

Railway Footbridges.

Stairs, Straight and Spiral.

This is a page from Mac Jarlane's catalogue of architectural castings.

The offices and works of A. & J. Main, founded in 1866, were located next door to the Saracen Foundry in Hawthorn Street. They were structural steel engineers as were many firms in this area - Brownlie and Murray, Fleming Brothers, Glasgow Steel Roofing, Lambhill Engineering and Kelvin Construction, all of which are now gone.

Main's covered a large area from Denmark Street to Ashfield Street and when they closed down in 1968, the whole site was converted into small industrial units. Fronting these was the Star Cash and Carry, which in time became the Paramount Bingo and is now Gala Bingo.

Possilpark Tram Depot was built for the Glasgow Corporation Tramways Department in 1900 and the last tram using this was the No. 18, Springburn to Shawfield on 3 June 1961. The depot is now used by buses of First Bus Company, who bought over Glasgow's bus services from Strathclyde Transport.

Next to the depot in Ashfield Street is Keppoch Park, the home ground of Glasgow Perthshire Football Club, founded in 1890, and this was their 1896 team. In 1932, 1941 and 1944, the 'Shire were the Scottish Junior Cup winners, overall champions in 1976/77, and twenty players have been capped for Junior international sides.

On the left is the 1930 Corporation housing scheme called Hawthorn, where all the streets are named after trees. The hedges surround the bowling greens of Hawthorn, the only private club left, as Possilpark of 1879 became defunct by 1985. The nearest public greens are in the parks of Ruchill and Springburn.

In the front centre of this very successful Ashfield FC side in 1928/29 was the fair-haired George Brown, a school teacher, who became a star with Rangers and Scotland. Ashfield's record in Junior competitions is outstanding, having won over 100 trophies with over 160 players turning professional to date. The home ground is Saracen Park, in Ashfield Stadium, where a record crowd of 26,513 attended a Scottish Cup tie in 1952-53 against Clydebank Juniors.

In 1949/50 this big mixed crowd cheered on the Ashfield Giants, their local speedway team, and especially their captain, Ken Le Breton, nicknamed the 'White Ghost'. Ken, an Australian, was one of the greatest riders this sport has ever produced and in his two years with Ashfield he won more trophies than any other rider. He was tragically killed in a racing accident in Sydney in 1951 and is still remembered by many fans in the northside.

There were many Clan Associations in Glasgow whose aims were to promote the Clan interests and sentiments by collecting and preserving records and traditions. Some of these had pipe bands which competed at Highland Games and Gatherings. This group the Clan Mackenzie Pipe Band, Possilpark, were photographed in about 1930 at the Isle of Bute Games and appear to have won a few trophies. The Possilpark connection, however, remains a mystery despite research.

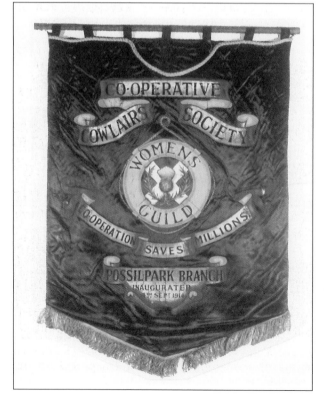

The Scottish Co-operative Wholesale Society, (SCWS), was abolished in the mid-seventies and the goodwill and trade were transferred to the CWS in Manchester. All of the Women's Guilds were disbanded and quite a few of their banners were given to local museums. Fortunately, Possilpark donated their banner to the People's Palace collection. The banner's background colour is purple with the lettering and design in blue, white and gold.

Six

Springburn

In the early nineteenth century, Springburn was a hamlet inhabited by weavers, quarry workers and farmhands. Dotted around were farms and country houses of Glasgow merchants and gentry. The decision to build the Edinburgh and Glasgow Railway, which opened in 1842, soon changed all this as the railway line went through the district and their workshops were located at Cowlairs. The company was taken over in 1865 by the North British Railway, and Cowlairs was greatly expanded. Another railway company, the Caledonian, erected their new workshops at St Rollox in 1856. Walter M. Neilson transferred his engineering factory in Hydepark Street, Anderston to Springburn, to build locomotives in 1862. Eventually this became part of the North British Locomotive Company in 1903 when Glasgow's three loco-builders amalgamated. Springburn had by that time become as famed for building locomotives as Govan had for ships. The boom in railway work meant that the population had increased rapidly and was housed in four-storey tenements. On Balgrayhill were villas for doctors, ministers and managerial staff. This close-knit community was shattered and scattered from around 1965 onwards, when the NB Loco went into liquidation, Cowlairs was closed down, heavy engineering went into decline and the Corporation of Glasgow started to implement their urban renewal programme. The latter was mainly for new roadways, which destroyed about 80 percent of the old tenements, replacing them with deck access housing and high rise flats, completely extinguishing that close community spirit of the past.

This is the erecting shop in the Hydepark Works of the North British Locomotive Company before the First World War. The company was the largest of its kind in Europe and exported most of its production to all parts of the world.

The Caledonian Railway Company decided in 1853 to move from its cramped workshops at Greenock and into new ones in the north side of Glasgow by 1854. The premises were called St Rollox and had situated within it the Glasgow and Garnkirk railway line of 1831. They were responsible for building, maintaining and repairing locomotives, coaches and goods wagons with a workforce of almost 4,000.

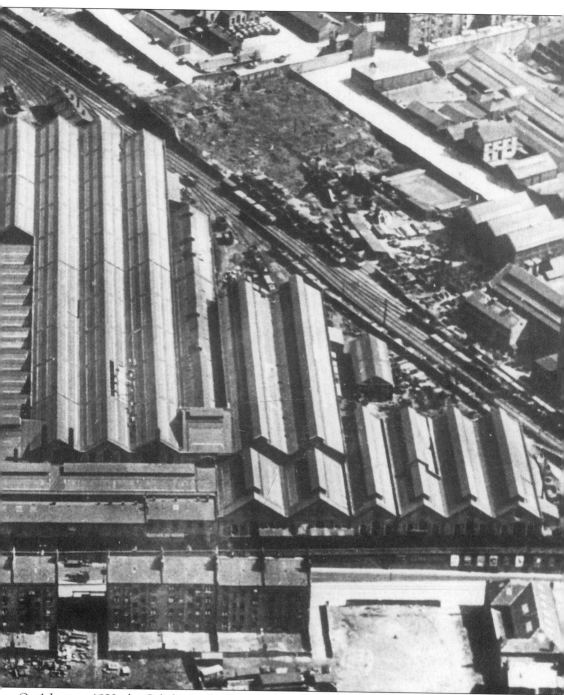

On 1 January 1923, the Caledonian Railway became part of the London Midland and Scottish Railway (LMS). The last locomotive of Caledonian design was completed in 1928 and thereafter the workers concentrated on maintenance and repair work. They became part of British Railways in 1948, and later British Rail Engineering Ltd. Gradually the workforce was reduced in numbers until it closed in 1990. Despite all the name changes, the works are still affectionately known as the 'Caley'.

This 1955 view shows the beginning of Springburn Road from the city centre. The bridge carried Glasgow's first railway line of 1831, the Glasgow and Garnkirk, which terminated further on at the St Rollox Chemical Works of Charles Tennant and Company. This bridge was demolished when the road was greatly widened. The workshops are that of Cowiesons Ltd, makers of wooden structures and warehouses and the others are the railway engineering ones of St Rollox.

Before the modernisation of Springburn Road for the heavy traffic of today, it had many twists and turns and this was the first, just beyond Petershill Road. Uphill, to the right, once led to the Labour Exchange,which has now been converted into flats. Adjacent to this was one of Springburn's picture houses called the New Kinema, nicknamed the 'Coffin' because of its shape and being over the wall from Sighthill Cemetery.

Springburn Fire Station on the left was built in 1893 and was vacated in 1986. The building was immediately converted into modern flats but the tenements shown beyond this were demolished to make new roadways to and from Bishopbriggs and beyond. The new fire station for Springburn is in Midton Street off Petershill Road.

The first electrically driven tramcars in Glasgow ran from Mitchell Street in the city centre to Keppochhill Road in Springburn and the inaugural day was 13 October 1898. These specially built ones were nicknamed the 'Room and Kitchen' and sometimes the 'But and Ben' ones, as they were divided into two saloons, separated centrally by a loading platform. The smoker's saloon had no window panes but had roller blinds for weather protection. The tramcar and the Keppochhill Road sheds are depicted in this early postcard.

Springburn Laundry, Keppochhill Road

Springburn Steam Laundry was converted from one of the vacant tramsheds in 1904. Their main workload initially was for the White House, a hostel in Ringford Street. Other users of the sheds were for joiners, glaziers, printers, car repairers and the Oxford cinema of 1927. The latter which was gutted by a fire on the New Years Day of 1941. Modern brick houses have now replaced all of these sheds.

Public Hall. Springburn.

Springburn Public Halls were opened on 10 May 1902 and this was another gift from Sir Hugh Reid of Hydepark Works. The architect was Wm. B. Whitie, who also designed the local library and the White House. The Halls were in regular use until the mid-fifties and were later converted into a sports centre which was never fully used. The vacant building is now below the high standards required for grant purposes so its future looks bleak.

The tram terminal in Keppochhill Road was at the public halls for the No. 4, Springburn to Renfrew and No. 16, Springburn to Whiteinch routes. In the days of colour coding, these trams were blue and green respectively. This one photographed in August 1950 has just crossed the bridge over the main railway line from Queen Street. In the early eighties the tenements on the left were renovated and refurbished whilst Sighthill church and the adjoining tenements on the right were razed for new roadways.

The junction of Keppochhill and Springburn Roads was always a busy one, used by at least four tram routes, Lawson's and Alexander's buses on the Kirkintilloch run and beyond. A new roadway bypasses Springburn hereabouts and the old tenements have been replaced by an attractive brick built one on a crescent which is floodlit at night.

A busy street scene of the early thirties with people (predominantly male) who seem to be waiting for a parade, or perhaps for the sight of a newly built locomotive on its way to Glasgow's docks from the nearby Hydepark Works. Springburn Road with Vulcan Street on the left and Cowlairs Road on the right, was called Springburn Cross at this junction.

Cowlairs junction was on the main line of the Edinburgh and Glasgow Railway since the opening of that company in 1842. It was from here that the line dropped at a gradient of 1 in 42 into the Queen Street terminal. Cowlairs was closed down in 1964, a couple of years before colsure of the adjacent railway workshops.

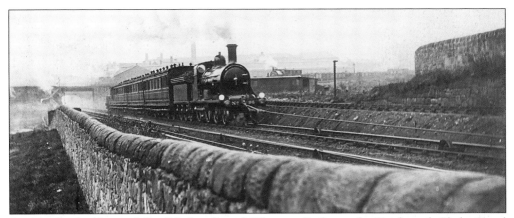

During the building of the Edinburgh and Glasgow Railway, the Forth and Clyde Canal proprietors objected to the plans for a bridge over the waterway. Consequently this meant tunnelling underneath it, very steeply, from Cowlairs to Queen Street Station. Ascending locomotives were helped by a rope attached to the front and hauled up by a stationary winding engine at Cowlairs. Brake vans were required for the descent and were also coupled there. This procedure became obsolete in 1908 when banking engines were used to assist.

BR Loco No. 60510, *Robert the Bruce*, descending the Cowlairs incline on 19 April 1952 and ascending later that day with the *Queen of Scots* Pullman for Edinburgh and King's Cross, London.

Cowlairs Estate was purchased by the Edinburgh and Glasgow Railway and in 1841 they established their railway workshops there. This was Springburn's beginning as one the great railway manufacturing centres in the world. In 1865 they were taken over by Scotland's biggest company, the North British, who decided that Cowlairs would be their principal workshop. Like the nearby St Rollox works, Cowlairs had excellent locomotive superintendents who were fiercely competitive of their rivals, as were the local workmen.

In the 1923 grouping of the railways, the North British became part of the London and North Eastern Railways, (LNER). They ceased to build locomotives the following year and continued to maintain and repair them and other rolling stock. In the 1948 nationalisation, Cowlairs became part of British Railways. In the early sixties, Dr Beeching swung his axe and Cowlairs was a casualty. The workload and some workers were transferred to St Rollox, which was then modernised. Despite protests and demonstrations, Cowlairs closed down in 1966. The prophecy that this was the death knell to railway engineering in Springburn proved to be correct.

The Railway Company, or the 'E and G' as they were fondly remembered, planned a model village for their workers. In 1863 they had built four blocks of houses in the Scots baronial style. Unfortunately, the company suffered financial difficulties and no more developments were scheduled.

These houses, or the 'Blocks' as they were known, lasted until 1967 and were replaced by a new housing scheme called Fernbank, which consisted of four-storey rows of deck access blocks, interjoined to each other. This design encouraged unsocial behaviour and ten years later they were altered to form more attractive and separate units.

Eastfield running sheds were just north of Cowlairs works and were built in 1904 by the North British Railways. They were badly damaged by fire on Saturday 28 June 1919. The sidings and sheds were great attractions for steam enthusiasts and train spotters. The top view shows LNER engines photographed on 29 July 1935, whilst the others are of British Railways No. 61924 (left) and No. 73103 (right), taken on April 1957 and May 1962 respectively.

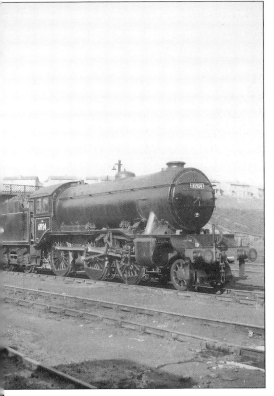

In 1949 Willie Gilmartin senior, photographed his workmates, Willie Hall, Johnny McLeod and Tam Redmond in the boiler shop of Hydepark Works. The noise must have been deafening and no ear protection was provided in those days. Some workers would stuff cotton in their ears to diminish the clamour.

In the erecting shop, at Hydepark works of the North British Locomotive Company Ltd, which was an amalgamation in 1903 of Glasgow's three locomotive builders - Neilson Reid of Hydepark, Sharp Stewart of Atlas and H. Dubs of Queen's Park. Their adminstration offices opened in 1908 and were in Flemington Street. These offices have now become the Springburn Campus of North Glasgow College.

This crowd of workers are not listening to a shop steward or concerned about an accident, they are watching the cards in the hands of the gambling school players during their dinner break. The card games played would be pontoons, brag or poker, side betting would be allowed in those days, 'way back in 1949'.

The NB Loco Company exported most of their production to Africa, South America, India and the Far East. Their journey from the works to the docks was always a commanding sight to witness. The 'big' crane at Stobcross Quay would load these engines onto a Clan or a City Line ship to be taken to all parts of the world. On the left is a type 2-8-2 bound for Mombasa on 14 June 1952 and the other is a type 2-8-2 on 19 September 1952, to be discharged at Port Sudan.

Springburn Cross, shown here in the early days of this century, is remarkably devoid of vehicular traffic but there are quite a few horse carts, including that of the local coalman who has stopped at the Vulcan Street corner. The building on the left is now modern flats and the shops have been converted into homes for pensioners. At one time, this building and all the shops belonged to Cowlairs Co-operative Society.

Carmichael's bakery and tearooms were very popular and their hall downstairs was often used for social occassions and receptions. It later became the premises of the local bookmaker, Charlie Tuck. Next door was Smith's Paint and Wallpaper Company, a haven for Springburn's handymen and DIY enthusiasts.

Springburn Railway Station, which can be seen between the tramcar and the end of the tenements on the left, was opened in 1887 for the City of Glasgow Union Railway suburban service. Today there is an electric service to Milngavie and a diesel service to Cumbernauld, both of which go through Queen Street station. The shops on the right are still occupied but the houses have been knocked down whilst the other side, after demolition, was used for the Parish Church and the Health Centre.

Sellyn's House of Fashion of 1958 is now a branch of a national bookmaker and the Savings Bank building, which is next to it, still survives as such. The ones opposite have all been destroyed and are now the Springburn Shopping Centre, a car park, a taxi stance and vacant space awaiting further developments. From Springburn Cross to the foot of Balgrayhill is called Springburn Way.

A 1952 view at the bottom of Balgrayhill, all of which has now completely disappeared except for the domed tenement at the hill-top. Fond memories are kindled by the City Bakeries tearooms wherein weddings, engagements and coming of age receptions were held.

Woolworths came to Springburn in the early fifties and closed down twenty years later when 'Woolies' was given a massive re-organisation which resulted in the closure of most stores in Glasgow, including all the city centre ones. This building became derelict and was demolished in the early nineties.

The demolition of these two-storey houses began in 1909. The area was levelled off to the main road and later became a children's playground. The bills are advertising seat letting in the local churches of Sighthill, Springburn North, St Rollox and Wellfield. Another notice is for a meeting in the Reid Hall on the Reform of the Fiscal System.

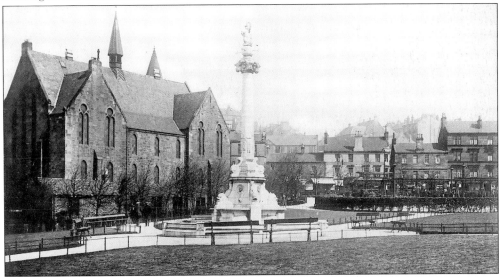

In 1912, Sir Hugh Reid, Managing Director of NB Locomotive Co., gifted money to create the Balgray Pleasure Grounds, which consisted of robust swings and roundabouts for children, an 'old men's shelter' and a little park with a white tiled Doulton fountain in the centre. Only the Unicorn column has survived the upheaval for new roadways and can now be seen in Springburn Park's floral display.

The Boys Brigade band escorts a Sunday School trip from Springburn North church in Elmvale Street in the summer of 1952. The weather forecast couldn't have been too bright as the men are all carrying or wearing their Mackintoshes. They would be joining up with a steam locomotive and carriages at the nearby Springburn Station to take them to their destination. Nowadays such outings use buses from door to door.

Every Sunday evening the Salvation Army Corps and Silver Band marched up Springburn Road from Gourlay Street to their Citadel in Wellfield Street. This was discontinued when the Corps moved into their new quarters in Fernbank Street in May 1968. They are posing here for a photograph in the mid-fifties where they were performing at Sunderland in a band contest.

Glasgow Corporation decided to run their own horse trams from 1 July 1894 when the lease which permitted the privately owned Glasgow Tramway and Omnibus Company to run on the municipal owned tramways had expired. Springburn's run was from the bottom of Balgrayhill to Mitchell Street in the city centre. They also introduced fares of one halfpenny for half-mile stages, which was held until 1920 when the minimum fare became a penny.

This pre-1920 postcard suggests that the Balgrayhill is the terminus. This is not correct as it was by then in Elmvale Street, where the blue No. 4a from Linthouse and the white No. 19 from Netherlee ended their journeys to Springburn. Occassionally the red No. 8 trams shortened their run here from Rouken Glen instead of going on to Bishopbriggs.

Earth moving equipment started in 1981 to change physically the land structure here for an elevated roadway over the dual carriageway of the new Springburn Expressway, which has now decimated the community. Wellfield United Presbyterian church lasted from 1899 until 1978, when the congregation united with most of the churches into Springburn Parish.

It is difficult to imagine that all of this 1958 scene has disappeared under rubble. The elevated roadway, which leads downhill to Hawthorn Street at Elmvale School, has been banked by grassy slopes and landscaped by shrubs and trees. Old Springburn, like the railway works, has completely vanished.

The No. 29 tramcar wends its way out to Bishopbriggs Cross, about 1½ miles distant, and the Cowlairs Co-op van has made a delivery to one of their 110 or so branches. At the corner opposite, was one of the area's favourite drinking holes, The Boundary Bar, which indicates that this was the first and the last pub in Springburn. Both the bar and all the Co-op shops are sadly missed.

Another successful season for the district's football team, Petershill Juniors, as Central League champions in 1932-33 season at their former Hawthorn Park. 'Peasy' were the Central League champions eleven times, Scottish Cup victors five times, and winners of numerous competitions. They celebrated their centenary in 1997 and according to their statistician and lifelong fan, Albert Moffat, they were just one trophy short of winning an honour for every year of their existence.

Springburn Park opened in 1892 and was laid out to the designs of the City Engineer, A.B. Macdonald. The cast iron bandstand was gifted the following year by James Reid, proprietor of Hydepark Works. The bandstand was manufactured at the nearby Saracen Foundry of Walter MacFarlane & Co, Possilpark. Both the aforementioned works and the bandstand have long since gone.

The Winter Gardens were erected in 1912 and were affectionately known as the 'Hothouses'. They were greatly visited, for inside were floral displays on the galleries and the winghouses, whilst tropical trees and ferns adorned the main hall. This was later converted into an exhibition area where shows and concerts were performed. Regrettably, the Winter Gardens are now in a state of disrepair.

The boating pond, photographed in the early thirties, was where young boys could sail their toy yachts and clockwork motorboats. Others could walk round the edge carrying a bamboo cane with a net attatched, which enabled children to fish for minnows. In the summertime they could hire and enjoy cranking paddleboats on the pond.

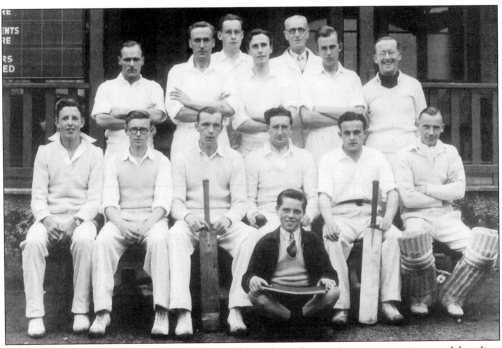

Sports activities were well catered for in the park with tennis courts, putting and bowling greens, football pitches and even a cricket pitch, all of these with their own pavilions. This shows the Cowlairs X1 in the summer of '49 ready for action in the field. Nowadays only bowls and football can be played as the other pitches have become open parkland.

New Mosesfield was built in 1838 for James Duncan, a bookseller in the Saltmarket. Later the house became the manse for Revd James A. Johnston of Springburn United Presbyterian church. Sir Hugh Reid purchased the lands and the house, gifting these to Glasgow Corporation for Springburn Park extensions in 1904. The ground floor became a museum and later an old men's club. The upper apartments are used as living quarters for the Parks Department staff.

This handsome villa, Belmont, was beside the park and commanded excellent views of the bordering countryside. It was commissioned in 1888 by Sir Hugh Reid and his bride, Marion Bell, the daughter of a wealthy merchant. Hugh was knighted in 1921 and died in 1935. He bequeathed the house to Stobhill Hospital as a children's home and nurses' quarters in memory of his wife, who had died in 1914. Because of vandalism and fires, the hospital management decided to demolish Belmont in 1985.

Stobhill Hospital was planned as a Poor Law establishment in 1899 and was fully operational when formally opened in September 1904. From the start of the First World War in 1914, the hospital was commandeered as the 3rd and 4th Scottish General hospital for wounded servicemen. Stobhill became a General Hospital in 1929 and continues to administer excellently to the needs of the surrounding populace.

At an early stage in the 1914-1918 War, hospital accommodation was inadequate so the Directors of the North British Locomotive Company permitted most of their administration offices to be converted into five convalescent wards. Named Springburn, Hydepark, Atlas, Queen's Park and Victoria, these wards were supervised by the Scottish Branch of the British Red Cross. Springburn Hospital, as it was then called, was ready for patients on Christmas Eve 1914 and had administered to the needs of 8,211 wounded when it closed in May 1919.

The open top tramcar in this early Edwardian postcard has just crossed the Glasgow boundary and into Bishopbriggs, to which a Sunday walk or tram ride was a popular destination for many Glaswegians in the summertime. The buildings on the left and the brick tenement in the centre have been demolished and the road is now much wider. The grasslands are now a large garage. The tenements and houses beyond are still standing.

Bishopbriggs was once a small village that prospered by the introduction through it of the Forth and Clyde canal around 1775 and the Edinburgh and Glasgow Railway's main line of 1842. Coal mining and sandstone quarrying were once the main industries. The population has exploded seven-fold since the 1951 census of 5,272. As many of them commute between here and Glasgow, there has been more roadway upheaval and changes to the face of Springburn.

Seven

North East

Much of this area was open countryside and farmlands, until the mid-twenties when the Corporation of Glasgow built the housing schemes of Riddrie, Blackhill, Provanmill and Balornock. In the post-war years, these extended to Broomfield and Barmulloch and in the mid-sixties the thirty one storey apartment blocks in the Red Road, the highest in Europe, were erected as well as other tower blocks of various heights. Of the industries, the biggest was the Provan gasworks and another was the Blochairn Steelworks. There were also a few brickworks and a large hospital at Robroyston, whose site was chosen because accommodation was needed for smallpox wards and to being four miles distant from the city centre and situated on high lying ground was considered suitable. The hospital grounds were of 54 acres and when these were sold off cheaply by the City Council, after the hospital's closure in mid-seventies, there was an uproar as the speculator sold off the lands to private building firms for millions of pounds. The Monkland canal which cut through Blackhill and Riddrie was filled in and became part of the M8 motorway which also took away much of the Blackhill housing scheme.

This is the presiding commitee of Robroyston Women's Co-op Guild accepting their banner from their guest of honour at a presentation dance c.1948. The Brigadoonish warrior depicted is possibly meant to be Sir William Wallace or perhaps it is that Scottish brigand, Rob Roy McGregor.

At the edge of Robroyston's newest housing estate is a Celtic Cross to the memory of Sir William Wallace. This was erected in 1900 to mark the site of the house in which Scotland's Braveheart was betrayed and captured on 5 August 1305.

The inscription continues, 'Wallace's heroic patriotism as conspicuous in his death as in his life, so roused and inspired his country that within nine years of his betrayal the work of his life was crowned in Victory . . . . on the field of Bannockburn.' There are other inscripted plates with quotes from Sir William Wallace and Robert Burns, Scotland's national poet.

A short walk further along from the monument is Wallace's Well, which is now enclosed by two stone walls with a path and steps leading to an opening similar to the one in this 1900 photograph. This has been renewed in pink granite stone with Wallace's Well engraved upon it, but it is not dated. Legend has it that Sir William Wallace refreshed his thirst at the well.

Blochairn Steelworks were part of the Steel Company of Scotland Ltd from 1880 to 1936, when they became a subsidary of Colvilles Ltd. They closed down in September 1962 and the cleared site was made into Blochairn Fruit market for Glasgow City Council in April 1969. The Fish Market was constructed alongside in 1977.

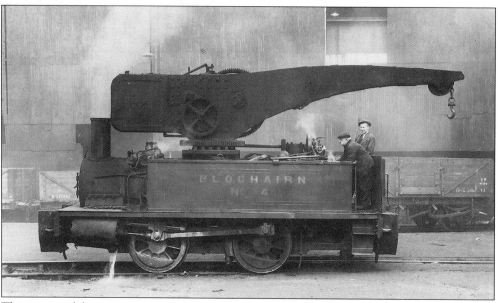

This crane tank locomotive, type 0-4-0, ran on a 3ft gauge railway within the steelworks, conveying ingots, scrap and other materials. No. 4 was manufactured at the Queen's Park Works of Henry Dubs and Company in 1881 and gave excellent service right up to the closure.

These furnaces were in the Plate Mill and steel ingots would be placed into them by the electric charging machine. They were taken out at the correct temperature and placed on to the rolling mills, which transformed the ingots into steel plates of various thicknesses.

When the steel plates were sufficiently cool, they were trimmed to the customer's requirements of length and breadth by those heavy plate shears. Test pieces were also required from each plate to determine material strength and when given a stamp of approval by Lloyd's inspectors, they would be transported by rail to the local shipyards, boilershops and engineering works.

Provan Gas Works, the largest belonging to the Municipality of Glasgow, were designed by Wm. Foulis, the Corporation's Gas Engineer, and completed after his death in 1903. They became the Scottish Gas Board, Glasgow Division, on the 15 May 1949. This 0-4-0 saddle tank industrial locomotive was manufactured at the nearby North British Locomotive's Hydepark Works in 1911 and scrapped in 1967.

This diminutive locomotive, type 0-4-0, and numbered 1, was built in 1946 by Andrew Barclay and Co. Kilmarnock and worked on a narrow gauge rail system of 2ft 6 in within the works. Their tasks were to convey rubbish from the retort ovens. This one was sold to Railway Enthusiasts Club, Farnborough, Hampshire in April 1962 and later resold to the Welshpool and Llanfair Light Railway, Montgomeryshire.

The narrow gauge locomotives, No.7 and No. 3, both of which were built by Andrew Barclay in 1916 and 1903 and scrapped in 1956 and 1960 respectively. Below is locomotive No. 4 built by the same makers in 1903 and scrapped in 1961. The Glasgow Council housing scheme of 1930 in the background is the discredited Blackhill, most of which has been knocked down to give access for the M8 motorway.

Glasgow Corporation procured Blackhill Golf Course for their housing schemes of Riddrie and Blackhill in the early twenties. The Glasgow Golf Club, which is the club's proper name, moved across the city to Killermont, just beyond the boundary at Maryhill, so technically the club is outside the city of its name.

Diagonally opposite the Blackhill Clubhouse and at the corner of Cumbernauld and Gartloch Roads, was the Cyclists Rest, an Italian cafe selling ice creams, light snacks and refreshments. This was later called the Golfers Rest because of the nearby Corporation golf course of Lethamhill. This scene was destroyed in the seventies for the M8 motorway approaches.

Hogganfield Loch was a pleasant day's outing for many as they strolled round, took a trip on the water by motor launch, hired out a rowing boat or pitched and putted on the course beside the tearoom. The island in the middle is a bird sanctuary.

Millerston, looking West.

Millerston was once a quiet little suburb as depicted in this 1910 scene with a church, cottages and and a country road with rhubarb fields on either side. The fields are now rows and rows of houses and the road is extremely busy with traffic in the morning and early evening. A new bypass has helped to lighten the road.

The phrase, 'Wish you were here', would be considered inappropriate if written on the backs of these two postcards of the thirties as one of them is HM Prison Barlinnie, (nicknamed the Bar-L), and the other is Riddrie Park Cemetery, which opened in 1904 and is now maintained by Glasgow's Parks Department.